Copyright ©2021 Charlene A. Ryan

All rights reserved. No part of this book may be reproduced or used in any manner whatsoever without written permission of the copyright owner except for the use of brief quotations in a book review.

First paperback edition September 2021

ISBN (paperback): 978-1-954041-10-3
ISBN (hardback): 978-1-954041-11-0

Published by Creative Sound Press
www.creativesoundpress.com
publishing@creativesoundpress.com

All book and cover art created with
oil on canvas by Charlene A. Ryan.
All rights reserved.

BIG and small Sounds

Charlene A. Ryan

*For Matthew, Aiden, Audrey Anna, and Amelia Claire.
May your lives be filled with beautiful moments, both
big and small.*

How to use this book

Each 2-page spread has unique combinations of artwork arranged in pairs of images that represent big and small sounds. They are basic and clear visual representations of loud and quiet sounds. The artwork also makes an excellent starting place for exploring the possibilities of the human voice. Encourage children to imagine the sounds that they hear in the images and how they might make those sounds using their voices. Ask them to consider what vocal sounds they could use, whether the sounds are big or small, and how they might create big or loud sounds and small or quiet sounds. And when you've exhausted the book's possibilities, have the children create their own artwork to represent their understanding, to further explore big and small sounds vocally, instrumentally, and using found sounds. Take it a step further and invite them to experiment with sounds that are not so loud, not so quiet, very loud, and very quiet. The possibilities are endless!

Crow is cawing in the night...

Seagull glides through fading light.

Crashing waves give quite a thrill...

Sunset glows on a sea so still.

Popping corn, a party delight...

Chocolate ice cream, cool and light.

Lips are sealed...

Now in laughter squeal...

Ripe bananas, soft and sweet...

Crunchy carrots, fun to eat.

Balloons float gently in the air...

Popping one gives quite a scare!

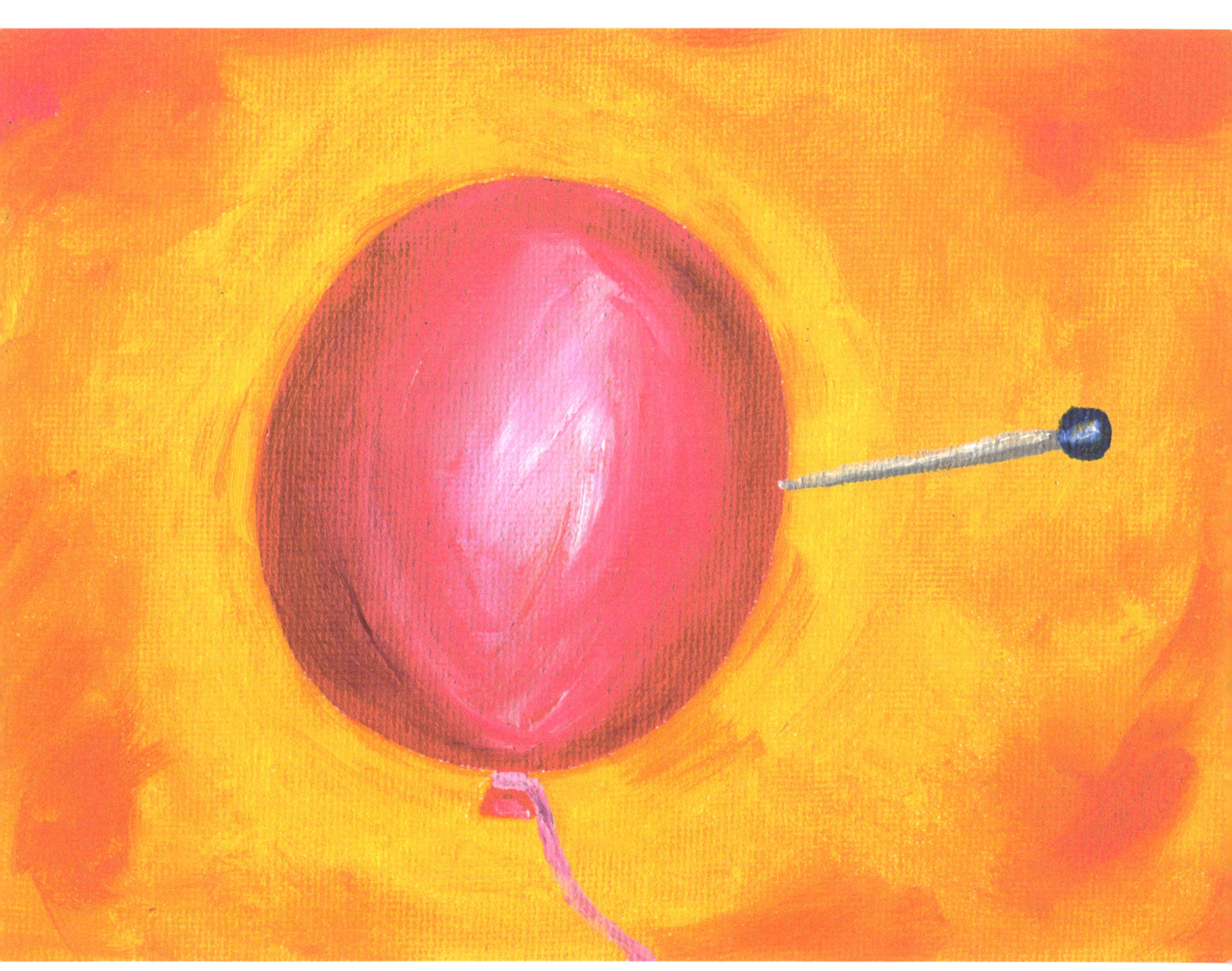

Butterfly flutters freely by...

Helicopter chops through the evening sky.

Honking horn can give a fright...

Triangle tings clear and bright.

Surprise! It's a party!

Shhhh! Don't wake the baby.

Lightning cracks through the darkened night...

A starry sky is a wondrous sight.

Fireworks – let's celebrate!

A candle glows upon the cake.

A storm so strong it bends the trees...

Snow sits softly without a breeze.

Charlene A. Ryan is a musician, painter, writer, and mom. She has spent most of her life behind an instrument and in front of an audience of one kind or another.

Other books by Charlene include:
Up and Down Sounds
Sections of Sound
Hannabelle's Butterflies
Katherine Lost

To learn more about Charlene and her work, visit www.charlenearyan.com

www.ingramcontent.com/pod-product-compliance
Lightning Source LLC
Chambersburg PA
CBHW041100070526
44579CB00002B/18